Summar

The Five Dysfunctions of a Team:

A Leadership Fable

By: Patrick Lencioni

Legal & Disclaimer

Legal & Disclaimer

The information contained in this book is not designed to replace or take the place of any form of medicine or professional medical advice. The information in this book has been provided for educational and entertainment purposes only.

The information contained in this book has been compiled from sources deemed reliable, and it is accurate to the best of the Author's knowledge; however, the Author cannot guarantee its accuracy and validity and cannot be held liable for any errors or omissions. Changes are periodically made to this book. You must consult your doctor or get professional medical advice before using any of the suggested remedies, techniques, or information in this book. Images used in this book is not the same as of that of the actual book. This is a totally separate and different entity from that of the original book titled: "The Five Dysfunctions of a Team"

Upon using the information contained in this book, you agree to hold harmless the Author from and against any damages, costs, and expenses, including any legal fees potentially resulting from the application of any of the information provided by this guide. This disclaimer applies to any damages or injury caused by the use and application, whether directly or indirectly, of any advice or information presented, whether for breach of contract, tort, negligence, personal injury, criminal intent, or under any other cause of action.

You agree to accept all risks of using the information presented inside this book. You need to consult a professional medical practitioner in order to ensure you are both able and healthy enough to participate in this program.

THE BOOK AT A GLANCE

The Five Dysfunctions of a Team by Patrick Lencioni is a **leadership** fable that explores the reasons **why** teams fail to function the way they **should**. It's the third book in a series of leadership fables that focuses on team dynamics. By using a **fictionalized** story of a promising company that has lost its way, Lencioni guides the readers to the **complex running of a team** in the hope of **identifying the issues** that hinder the team from achieving its goals.

Lencioni presents the five dysfunctions of a team by using a **fable** so readers can have a better **grasp** of concepts and theories as they are applied to the **fictional** company. The book is split into **two major sections**: *The Fable* and *The Model*.

The Fable is presented in **four parts** representing the **major story arcs** that introduce the fable and the main characters in the story.

In Part One, the story is set up by introducing **DecisionTech**, touted as the most **promising** start-up company in Silicon Valley. It gives the backstory of how such a **well-funded** company could stumble and fall quickly. It **outlines** the events that transpired which led to the company's fall from grace and eventual demotion of its co-founder and CEO. This section also introduces **Kathryn, the new CEO** who has the unenviable **task of leading a dysfunctional team.** The team consists of different individuals with **clashing personalities**, which makes Kathryn's task even more difficult. Team members are introduced by stating their backgrounds, company positions and key personal traits that affect the team dynamics.

In Part Two, the **issues and troubles** in the team unravel. This section gives us a glimpse into how the team members **behave** in meetings. It shows how Kathryn handles the first few days of her job as the new CEO and how she was met with **defiance and doubts**. It also presents what transpires in the meetings, which shows how dysfunctional the team is. **Theories and concepts** about team dynamics are presented through Kathryn's point of view. The **five dysfunctions and their causes** are presented and explained and their application is tested in a series of team activities.

In Part Three, Kathryn experiences the **deterioration** of the progress the team managed to accomplish. It presents the **bigger challenges** the team faces and how each team member **reacts** to Kathryn's every action. This is also where the personality clashes become more explosive.

In Part Four, the story takes a more somber tone as it presents the **changes and the transformations** the team experiences under Kathryn's leadership.

The second section of the book explains in detail the **theories and principles** behind the five dysfunctions of the team. It also lists the ways how to **overcome** the problems and how to assess the team.

The Conclusion summarizes the incredible **insights** and the lessons learned from the fable and how readers can benefit from this book. It also recapitulates the **main** points of the story and reiterates the importance of **applying** the lessons in real-world scenarios.

INTRODUCTION

Author Patrick Lencioni believes the **real competitive advantage** of an organization is **teamwork**. Many organizations fail to acknowledge this. They look for the problems in processes and strategies and come up with solutions that only solve the symptoms and not the **underlying cause** of the problem. They do recognize the importance of teamwork, but they have this **notion that their teams are functioning well**. They have no idea most of the problems they face stem from having a dysfunctional team.

In this day and age, it is a rarity to find a team that's operating to its **full potential**. Most teams are broken and beset by countless problems. If nothing is done to fix them, they will continue to function **inefficiently and ineffectively**, much to the detriment of the team and the organization as a whole.

If people in the organizations work as a **team** and have a **clear understanding** of the goals then it's possible to dominate any industry at any time. Many team leaders and managers would have no trouble agreeing to this. The difficult part is making it happen. It's **difficult** because leaders have to deal with **individuals** who are **inherently dysfunctional**. The issues are not just about work processes and strategies, but **attitudes** and **behaviors**.

Great teamwork is elusive but it does not mean it's impossible to achieve. It requires mastering certain behavior patterns that seem uncomplicated theoretically but are very difficult to put into practice. If teams can overcome their negative behavioral tendencies, then half of the battle is won. The other half is about **applying the principles and theories** and making sure they stick.

Like the other books that are included in the leadership fable series, *The Five Dysfunctions of a Team* starts off with a story of a fictional organization plagued by **realistic problems**. By creating a story, readers can easily **relate** to the scenarios and the characters. This helps them understand the theories better because they have real-world applications. The complex theories and concepts are broken down into chunks that are easily digested. This can help readers get an idea of how the principles are **put into practice**. This way, they can replicate the approaches that work and avoid the behaviors that contribute to the problem.

The book **balances** the theories and the applications so it comes out as a **cohesive** story with insights and lessons. To make the **retention** rate even better, the second part of the book reintroduces the five dysfunctions and provides different solutions to overcome these dysfunctions.

In all of these, the **role of leaders becomes crucial** in the process of transforming teams and organizations. They have the **responsibility** of guiding the team in the direction it has to go. In order to do that, the leaders need to **master the principles** and know how to apply them. This means the change must start with them.

This book serves as a **tool** to help leaders **start the process** of transformation in their respective teams. It would also benefit individuals who are part of an organization and a team. Even though the story centers on a tech startup in Silicon Valley, it doesn't mean the application is only limited to one area of business. The principles, theories, ideas, and insights in this book **can be applied to other fields where teams exist.** It can be used by non-profit organizations, charitable institutions, church groups, sports teams, and educational institutions, to name a few.

The Five Dysfunctions of a Team is practical guide that also provides **actionable steps** to overcome the problems. Reading this book can help fix the problems in teams so they can have the best chance of succeeding even in the face of challenges.

FREE BONUSES

P.S. Is it okay if we overdeliver?

Here at Readtrepreneur Publishing, we believe in overdelivering way beyond our reader's expectations. Is it okay if we overdeliver?

Here's the deal, we're going to give you an extremely condensed PDF summary of the book which you've just read and much more…

What's the catch? We need to trust you… You see, we want to overdeliver and in order for us to do that, we've to trust our reader to keep this bonus a secret to themselves? Why? Because we don't want people to be getting our exclusive PDF summaries even without buying our books itself. Unethical, right?

Ok. Are you ready?

Firstly, remember that your book is code: "**READ97**".

Next, visit this link: http://bit.ly/exclusivepdfs

Everything else will be self explanatory after you've visited: http://bit.ly/exclusivepdfs.

We hope you'll enjoy our free bonuses as much as we enjoyed preparing it for you!

THE FABLE

LUCK

Kathryn Petersen inherited DecisionTech, Inc., a start-up company that has **fallen from grace** just two years after it was touted as the most promising tech company in Silicon Valley. Kathryn took the **reins as CEO** with all-out support from the Chairman of the board. She couldn't have known how **dire** the situation was in DecisionTech and it was up to her to fix it.

PART ONE: UNDERACHIEVEMENT

BACKSTORY

DecisionTech was not part of Silicon Valley geographically because of its location in Half Moon Bay, which is a coastal farming town south of San Francisco, but the company fits within the Silicon Valley culture perfectly. The location did not matter to venture firms who lined up to invest in the company. With an experienced executive team and a **shatter-proof business plan**, DecisionTech was <u>**primed to succeed**</u>. The first few months of operations showed tremendous promise, but it didn't take long for the **cracks** in the company to show. Key personnel left unexpectedly, deadlines were slipping off, and the employee morale took a nosedive.

In the company's second year, 37-year-old CEO Jeff Shanley was asked to step down but was offered a job to head the business development unit. Jeff agreed to the demotion because he didn't want to miss out on the potentially huge payout if the company went public.

Jeff was liked by the 150 employees, but they couldn't deny the fact that his leadership created an **atmosphere of divisiveness**. Discord among executives became commonplace. Without a sense of commitment and team unity, everything took so long to finish. The company was wasting away because of **company politics**. The board could not afford bad publicity, but the company had already developed a reputation within Silicon Valley for being an **unpleasant place to work**. Three weeks later **Kathryn Petersen** was hired as the **new CEO**.

KATHRYN

Kathryn Petersen had no solid experience running a tech company. The only involvement she had with a startup was being a board member of Trinity Systems, a San Francisco-based company. Her career experience had been largely taking on **operational roles** in manufacturing companies, the most notable of which was an auto manufacturer.

At 57 years old, she was considered ancient. In fact, she already retired from work three years prior. She started her career in the military, married a teacher, and raised three boys. Nothing about her seems to match the culture of DecisionTech but Kathryn had an **affinity for business**. She completed a three-year business school night program which eventually landed her different jobs in the manufacturing sector.

Interestingly, her being a **woman** was never an issue. High-tech companies at Silicon Valley are relatively more gender progressive so having women in the management team was nothing unusual. The bigger issue was the **glaring cultural mismatch**. Kathryn's background and old-school management style were a **stark contrast** to DecisionTech's management team which consisted of executives and middle managers who had little experience outside of Silicon Valley.

Despite the **mismatch**, the Chairman of the board convinced the board members Kathryn was the best choice to lead the company. DecisionTech was desperate and there was a **dearth of qualified executives** willing to fix the mess. The Chairman argued that the board members should consider themselves lucky to have a capable leader run the ailing business. A few weeks after Kathryn was hired, the Chairman **regretted his decision**.

RATIONALE

The job offer was a surprise to Kathryn. She had known the Chairman on a personal level and they had been friends for a long time. It never occurred to her that the Chairman thought highly of her as an executive and as a leader. Their relationship had been largely on a social level centering on family and school life since her husband taught the Chairman's oldest son in high school.

Unbeknownst to Kathryn, the Chairman had followed her career over the years and was **impressed** at how **successful** she had become with modest training. She was known for **building amazing teams** within the company. Her achievements were remarkable in that she had become a chief operating officer of a successful automobile manufacturing plant, which was a US-Japan joint venture. In fact, the company was listed as one of the most **successful enterprises** in the country during her stint. This was enough to convince the Chairman that Kathryn had what it took to fix DecisionTech's mounting problems.

GRUMBLINGS

It was obvious the decision to hire Kathryn was **met with doubts** but it was the first two weeks that made the executives more **defiant**. It was not because she changed things around, but it was the fact that Kathryn was **doing nothing**. She would spend most of the time **silently observing meetings** and **chatting up with the staff**. The most controversial move she made was to actually let her predecessor Jeff lead the weekly executive staff meetings. She just sat there and took notes.

The only action Kathryn took was to announce **executive retreats** in Napa Valley. This boggled their minds because the last thing they needed was time away from work when there were so many things to be done. No one was more shocked than the Chairman. He decided if things would not work out with Kathryn, the best thing to do was to leave along with her.

OBSERVATIONS

Two weeks into her role as CEO of DecisionTech, Kathryn wondered if she should have accepted the job in the first place. Then she realized retirement made her antsy and there was little chance she would have declined the offer. She welcomed the new challenge. However, DecisionTech was a completely different challenge for her and the **prospect of disappointing** the Chairman **frightened** her just a little bit. Although she was very confident in herself, she still worried that failure could tarnish her reputation so late in her career. **It was not the legacy she wanted to leave behind**.

Kathryn believed she would be able to turn things around for the failing company, but all she needed was a little **more time and leeway**. She refused to be intimidated by the **yuppies** in the company. She was so self-assured that her lack of in-depth software experience was not a concern to her. She even thought of it as an advantage because the software experts were just completely **paralyzed by their own knowledge of technology**. She believed what she knew of enterprise software was enough for her to lead the company to success. What Kathryn was not prepared for was how **dysfunctional** the executive team was and how they **defied her relentlessly** in ways she had never experienced before.

THE STAFF

It was no accident that employees referred to the executives of DecisionTech as The Staff. **No one referred to them as a team**. The Staff consisted of highly intelligent individuals with very impressive educational backgrounds. However, they showed little of that in their meetings. There was no apparent open hostility and there were no heated arguments, but the tension was undeniable. During meetings, **discussions were slow** because there were only a few exchanges of ideas. No one seemed **interested** in being in there.

JEFF—FORMER CEO, BUSINESS DEVELOPMENT

Jeff Shanley was key in raising a substantial amount of money for DecisionTech. His **expertise in venture capital and recruiting** was what attracted the current executives to the company. His management skills were another story.

Jeff facilitated staff meetings as though he were a student body president. Everything was prepared and minutes of the meeting were distributed after. The fact that nothing got done **didn't bother him**.

MIKEY— MARKETING

Michelle "Mikey" Bebe's great reputation as a **brand-building genius** was well-known in Silicon Valley, so everyone on the board was ecstatic when she joined the company. The only problem was she **complained a lot** during meetings. She talked more than the others and would come up with some amazing ideas, but they were outnumbered by her complaints. It was her **lack of social graces** that was off-putting. Despite her enormous talent and accomplishments, she was the least popular in the team – except for Martin.

MARTIN—CHIEF TECHNOLOGIST

Martin Gilmore was a **co-founder** of the company. He was the closest thing the company ever got to having an inventor. He single-handedly designed the original specs for DecisionTech's flagship product, but other people had done the actual product development. He was considered as the company's most **valuable human capital** because of his track record.

Martin was not disruptive during meetings, but he **rarely participated**. He constantly checked his emails and was engrossed in other activities. His peers **tolerated** him and his sarcastic remarks because they held him in high regard. With the company's struggles, it became a **source of frustration** for his colleagues.

JR—SALES

Jeff "JR" Rawlins was the **head of sales**. As an experienced sales person, it was strange he **rarely followed through**. He did acknowledge that some commitments were not fulfilled as expected. He apologized profusely to people he had let down. Because of this, he was able to maintain a bit of respect from his colleagues. Curiously, RJ had **never** missed a quarterly revenue target before coming to work for DecisionTech.

CARLOS—CUSTOMER SUPPORT

Although the company didn't have many customers, the board decided to invest in customer service in preparation for its anticipated growth. They hired Carlos Amador, a former colleague of Mikey. The two personalities couldn't be more **different**. Carlos was the quiet type, but when he spoke, he contributed something important. He was also **constructive** in his approach. He was **low-key** and he **worked long hours without complaints.**

JAN—CHIEF FINANCIAL OFFICER

Jan Mersino's role as CFO had been crucial to the company's operations. Jan knew what she signed up for and she played a supporting role to Jeff. The board **trusted** Jan to not let things get out of hand, especially since the other executives were given a **free rein** when it came to spending.

NICK—CHIEF OPERATING OFFICER

On paper, Nick Farrel's **credentials** were very **impressive**. He had been VP of field operations for a large computer manufacturing company in the Midwest prior to joining DecisionTech. He got the position because he had demanded the title as a condition of accepting the job. Hence, his **responsibilities were ill-defined**.

With the change in leadership, Nick's **responsibilities were put on hold**. He didn't openly complain, instead, he built relationships with his colleagues. He believed he was the only person qualified to run the company as CEO.

PART TWO: LIGHTING THE FIRE

FIRST TEST

Kathryn had been on the job for a while when she received a message addressed to everyone in the executive team. It was from Martin, the company's chief engineer. He wanted to let everyone know he and JR would be meeting with ASA Manufacturing during the same week of the executive retreat. This did not sit well with Kathryn so she decided to **confront** Martin and tell him he had to **reschedule the meeting** with the client because the **retreat was the first priority**.

Not used to being contradicted and confronted, Martin became **agitated** and countered that Kathryn had her priorities confused. Kathryn insisted they should **get their act together** and there would be no selling until that happened. Martin did not respond, but at that moment he knew the fight was not yet over.

END RUN

Jeff mustered enough courage to raise the issue that had prompted the lunch invitation to Kathryn. Jeff opened up the topic of Martin's ASA meeting coinciding with the retreat. Jeff sided with Martin that the customer meeting was more important than the internal meeting. However, Kathryn was adamant and reiterated that she was hired to make things work in the organization. **She was intent on straightening out the leadership problem in the company.** Jeff decided any further discussion would be futile and possibly career-breaking, so he let it go.

DRAWING THE LINE

Kathryn was **unfazed** by the talk she had with Jeff. She had anticipated some form of **backlash** about the incident with Martin, but she didn't expect it to come from the Chairman himself.

The Chairman raised his concerns and said Kathryn was already **setting things on fire even before building bridges.** Kathryn didn't mince words and said the things she was doing were **intentional and purposeful** and would help the company get out of the rut it was in. She insisted that a fractured team needs fixing and that it was not going to be easy. The decisions were definitely not popular with the team, but it was a **necessary evil**.

NAPA

Everyone **except** Martin arrived at Napa Valley by 8:45 in the morning, just in time for the 9:00 AM meeting. No one said anything about Martin, but they wondered if he would be on time or if he would be there at all. Even Kathryn was a little bit nervous because the last thing she wanted to do was **reprimand** someone for being late. They all breathed a sigh of relief when Martin arrived at 8:59.

THE SPEECH

During the meeting, Kathryn reminded the team that DecisionTech had the most **talented team** of any of their competitors. She also mentioned that the company was more **liquid** and had the **better technology** compared to tech companies operating in the same field. With all these advantages, the company was **still behind in terms of revenue and customer growth.** She then asked the team why but was only answered with deafening silence.

Kathryn told everyone the problem was that the executive team was **not functioning as a team.** The tension was palpable because everyone shot glances at Jeff waiting for his reaction. Kathryn picked up on this so she said this was not a stab at Jeff or anyone else.

Kathryn continued with her speech and let everyone know there would be **big changes** including possibly letting go of people who were not the best match for the company. She assured everyone the only reason why they were in Napa was to **achieve results**. She expected the company would get back on track and achieve growth and profitability, guarantee customer satisfaction and retention, and possibly start an **IPO**.

Kathryn then discussed the first reason why teams are dysfunctional.

Absence of Trust

Trust is the cornerstone of teamwork. Without it, the team would not perform efficiently. Team members should be able to **admit** their mistakes and their weaknesses **without fear of judgment or reprisal**. It was clear from the start that the executives did not trust one another so it was an issue that needed to be addressed.

PUSHING BACK

Although things were starting to make sense, Jan and the rest of the team started to ask questions which Kathryn answered somewhat convincingly. She mentioned that all her findings were based on data she pulled from months of observing the team. She concluded that the team **lacked passionate discussion or debate**. Mikey said it was because there was just not enough time to argue. Jeff didn't agree and said everyone was not comfortable challenging others during meetings. Mikey countered that perhaps it was because the meeting was too boring and structured. Nick spoke up and said the problem was that the team members couldn't and didn't agree on anything.

Kathryn said the team had **trust issues**. For the first time, some members agreed with Kathryn. Martin completely zoned out of the lively conversation and started banging away at his keyboard, which distracted everyone in the room. Kathryn knew this was her moment to **prove her point**.

ENTERING THE DANGER

The **tension mounted** as Kathryn watched Martin type away at his keyboard. Kathryn then made her move and asked him if he was working on something with just enough sarcasm to provoke a response. Martin said he was taking down notes. Kathryn reiterated that her rules for meetings were simple and that they just needed to be **present** and **participate** in the discussion. She demanded that they be **engaged**. Martin pulled back and joined the discussion as a conciliatory move. Kathryn was starting to get everyone's attention.

GETTING NAKED

After the **"icebreaker"**, the first real exercise of the meeting was to **share personal histories** by answering five **nonintrusive** personal questions about their backgrounds. One by one, the executives provided answers. They learned new things about each other that were outside of the four walls of the company. They were amazed at the personal disclosures:

Mikey studied ballet at the prestigious Juilliard School in New York. Carlos had eight siblings and he was the oldest. Jeff was once a bat boy for the Red Sox. JR had a twin brother. Jan was a military brat. Martin spent his childhood in India. Nick was a basketball player and played against Kathryn's husband's team.

After 45 minutes of sharing personal information, the team appeared to be more at ease with each other. Of course, Kathryn **expected the euphoria to diminish** once the discussion switched back to serious topics.

GOING DEEPER

After the short break, the team had already lost their glow from the fun morning session. They spent the better part of the afternoon answering **diagnostic tools to determine their behavioral tendencies**. One of the tools was the Myers-Briggs Type Indicator.

It was clear that everyone liked learning and talking about themselves, but they **didn't like listening to criticism**. It was going to come but Kathryn decided to do that when everyone had taken a long break to energize themselves.

At dinnertime, the team was still in good spirits and was able to pick up the conversation from where they left off. They had **acknowledged** the differences in their personalities and the **implications** of being an extrovert and an introvert. They were loosening up but getting a little deeper into the conversations.

Kathryn was **amazed** at the progress they had **achieved** in just a short time. It was better than she could have imagined given the circumstances. The team was finally willing to talk about the dysfunctional behaviors observed by Kathryn.

Among the executives, it was Mikey who opened the door to her own issues. When Nick made a remark about how accurate the personality descriptions were, Mikey just rolled her eyes. Nick didn't fail to notice it and asked her point blank what it was about. Mikey acted like she didn't do anything. Jan called her out on her behavior. Mikey admitted that she was not into psychobabble.

The team shifted to business-related discussion and linked the operational issues with behavioral ones. It became clear to Kathryn that Mikey's did not **trust** her colleagues.

POOLSIDE

After the session ended, Kathryn went to talk to Mikey to see if she could make some progress with her. Mikey felt like she was **made fun of** and she did not like it one bit. Clearly upset, Mikey said her colleagues didn't know **how** to make DecisionTech successful. This caught Kathryn off-guard because she didn't know what brought on that response. Kathryn said they could talk about it, but Mikey quickly said the team was not going to hear from her.

REBOUND

Mikey was in good spirits on the second day of the meeting. She looked unfazed and even seemed **enthusiastic** following the previous day's events. The team went over the materials they had covered the day before but Martin, Nick, and JR became bored and distracted. Kathryn reminded everyone they were **reviewing** what they had learned the previous day because repetition would help the lessons stick. However, the most important exercise of the day was something that would be the **moment of truth** for the entire executive team.

AWARENESS

Kathryn explained that for teamwork to start, there should be trust. Building trust means **overcoming the need for invulnerability**. She asked everyone to list what they thought their **strengths and weaknesses** were. She started the discussion rolling when she shared that her strength was her ability to see through superfluous information and get through to the things that mattered. She acknowledged that she was not good at speaking in public.

Each of the executives shared their strengths and weaknesses in a lively discussion that pleased Kathryn. The fact that everyone was participating was a breakthrough for a team that didn't want the meeting in the first place. Even Mikey participated but she was not as open as the rest of the guys.

Things got a little uncomfortable when Mikey reacted to Nick's strength and weakness and said he was just an arrogant S.O.B just like every chief technology officer in Silicon Valley. Although it was said in jest, no one laughed. Nick was melting inside. Kathryn regretted not calling out Mikey for her tactless remark. She concluded that Mikey had a **low emotional intelligence** and her **lousy behavior** was affecting everyone in the team in a bad way.

EGO

Kathryn discussed the next dysfunction called *inattention to results.* Members of the team tended to **seek individual recognition at the expense of results.** Individual ego had a place on the team, but it should not have been greater than the **collective ego**. If everyone was focused on achieving the goals and reaching the results that they aimed for, it would be difficult for the individual ego to get out of hand.

To echo the guiding principle that her husband followed in his coaching career, Kathryn explained that the goal was to **create the best team possible** and **not shepherd the careers of individuals** in the team.

Athletes who play in team sports have massive egos but they are usually **tied to a result**. The result is winning. Although athletes like getting into an All-Star team or getting multi-million endorsement deals, they like winning more. If a team consists of people who only look out for themselves, then success is hard to reach.

Mikey asked what all the sports discussion had to do with a software company. Kathryn explained that the concept could be applied to their company in that their **collective results** should be regarded as **important** as a score in a sports game. When everyone is clear about the importance of the collective results, then there's **no opportunity for individual egos to creep in.**

Mikey countered that the company already had a scoreboard in the form of profit. Kathryn clarified that **profit** was a big part of the result, but it was **not the only result**. If the company let profit be the only guide, it wouldn't know the team performance before the profit numbers were disclosed.

The team's job was to **define the goals or the results** that needed to be achieved in simple terms that were specific enough to be **actionable**. Profit was not actionable enough so it needed to be related to what the team did on a daily basis. Kathryn then challenged the team to come up with a clearly defined goal.

GOALS

The executive team was broken into smaller groups and they were asked to propose a **list of results categories** that could be the team's scoreboard in the medium term. They decided on revenue, expenses, new customer acquisition, current customer satisfaction, employee retention, market awareness, and product quality. These categories were to be **measured monthly** so that it would be easier to **detect problems** and find **immediate solutions** for them.

Martin and JR commented that the metrics were nothing new and were, in fact, the same metrics that the company has been using for nine months. Kathryn was amused at the **predictability** of the team. As soon as they shifted to real business problems, the team members **returned to their old behaviors** that put them in a predicament.

Kathryn then asked what the company's PR goal was and the team could not give a straight answer. The team dynamics were once again disturbed with one member **blaming** the other. Martin and Mikey got into an argument about marketing and sales. Mikey went in defensive mode and told everyone the company's problems are not due to marketing. She even said her department had done a remarkable job considering what they had to work with. And just like that, the conversation came to a screeching halt.

DEEP TISSUE

Kathryn reiterated to the group that the team should focus on the **results** instead of **individual recognition**. The team should adopt a set of **measurable common goals** and use them to make a collective decision on a day-to-day basis. She was able to prove a point when no one could give **specific** answers when she asked a series of questions about goal setting, metrics, and inter-department effort.

Jeff explained that when he was CEO, he let the department heads be accountable for their own actions in their own areas of expertise. Kathryn used a sports analogy to show that every member of the team should know what the other was talking about so that they could function as a team. Otherwise, they were just a bunch of individuals doing their own thing. This meant **everyone was responsible** for sales, finance, marketing, product development, and customer service. The truth and simplicity of the analogy made the team realize how inadequate they were as a team. The **unity** that they thought they had was just an **illusion**.

Things got heated up when Kathryn said the **politics** in the team astounded her. The **ambiguity** of each one's goals made it easy for individuals to focus on their **own** success and not on the team's success. The team completely disagreed with her. They didn't think they were political at all. They then saw an opportunity to challenge Kathryn. Mikey was the most hostile when she said giving that kind of remark after just a few weeks was careless.

Kathryn apologized but she made sure that she was still in control of the group. She'd rather overstate the problem than downplay it because it was a way to help the company go where it needed to go.

Nick was confused and asked what Kathryn meant by politics. She explained that it's when **people speak and act based on how they want others to react instead of on how they actually think.** With that definition, Martin said the team was **definitely** political.

Kathryn was still unsure if the team would embrace her ideas, but it quickly became clear that the team would attack her ideas.

ATTACK

Of all the team members, it was JR who surprisingly challenged Kathryn. He said he could not wait for three weeks to find out what the other three dysfunctions were so he asked her to just tell them what was not working so they could get on with it.

Kathryn wanted to reveal the three other dysfunctions gradually, but she decided to heed JR's advice to go through them right at that moment.

EXHIBITION

Kathryn explained that trust was necessary because, without it, the team would not be able to engage in an **open and constructive conflict**. Without this healthy conflict, the team was just preserving an **artificial unity and harmony**, which did not help solve company problems. Nick challenged her and said the team already had plenty of conflicts and not a lot of harmony. Kathryn corrected him and said what they had was **tension**. She added that the team had no real constructive conflict. **Passive comments** and **sarcastic** ones were not the kinds of conflict that were required to make the team function well.

The reason why there was no constructive conflict was because the team had a *fear of conflict,* which was the next type of dysfunction. That was why they **held back their honest opinions** and were **unable to communicate the real issues** that plagued the company.

Martin was not convinced and said more arguments just take up a lot of time and would not accomplish anything. Amazingly, this prompted the other team members to join in the discussion and they even defended Kathryn's logic. Jan was a little more vocal and said not being able to hash things out was more of a waste of time.

The next dysfunction that Kathryn revealed was *lack of commitment,* which includes the inability to buy in to decisions. **Ambiguity** is the evidence of this lack of commitment. Kathryn explained that if people didn't communicate their opinions, they would not **commit to a decision**. No one is forced to support a particular effort, but people should make a case why they are not supporting that effort. And that is when constructive conflict starts. In general, reasonable people don't really need to have their way in any meeting or discussion, but they want their input **acknowledged** and **responded to**.

The last dysfunction is *avoidance of accountability*. When a team obtains **clarity** of the results it wants to achieve, it will commit to a decision. Once a collective decision is arrived at, team members should hold each other **accountable** for the decision they made as a **team**.

The executives agreed that this was difficult because it brought interpersonal discomfort. The act of calling someone out and telling him or her that their performance is sub-par is something that many people try to avoid. It's harder to do with peers because there's this notion that as peers, they're supposed to be equals. However, the one issue that makes team accountability difficult is *not buying in*. This is because when team members don't buy in to a decision, they could just **easily** say that they never agreed to it in the first place.

FILM NOIR

Kathryn acknowledged that it was **difficult** to break through the wall that the team had built. The behavioral problems that stemmed from too much politics were hard to correct. **Changes can't just happen overnight**. Although her lectures were compelling enough to make the team pay attention and shift their way of thinking slightly, Kathryn felt there was still a lot of heavy lifting to be done.

The discussion switched back to conflict. Conflicts happen in meetings. If team members cannot engage in the **productive** exchange of ideologies, then it's pointless to have these meetings. The ability to engage in **passionate debates** determines the future of the company because it is where great ideas come up and products are conceptualized.

Kathryn compared being in a meeting to watching a movie. They both run for 90 minutes. In meetings, there is **interaction** while in movies, there is no interaction. Movies have no impact on real life while **meetings** are relevant and sometimes even **crucial**. Based on this comparison, meetings should be interesting and people should be attending them instead of dreading them.

However, every good movie has one key element and that is **conflict**. Without conflict, no one cares what happens to the characters. In the same vein, meetings without conflicts will not make the attendees care. With that poignant introduction, Kathryn opened the floor for the team's first **substantive** decision-making session.

APPLICATION

Kathryn wanted to **establish the overarching goal** of the team for the rest of the year. It was the goal they needed to accomplish between then and the end of the year. Evidently, there was **no consensus** because each of the members had a **different priority** in mind. With different opinions presented, the team started to have a **constructive conflict.** Although they couldn't agree on one thing, some of them conceded to reasons provided. Kathryn was pleased because it was the first time the team engaged in a productive conversation.

Kathryn wanted the team to have a consensus in the next five minutes so she asked everyone to make a passionate plea for the goal they supported. For every goal that was raised, some members talked themselves out of the answer so the choices were **narrowed down** significantly.

Carlos provided the most compelling argument that customer acquisition was the best choice because he believed that it would give the press something good to write about the product, which in turn would build employee confidence. Since there would be more customers, they could provide feedback to the engineers on how to improve the product.

For the first time, the team came to a **collective decision**. Kathryn wanted to be more specific so she initiated a debate on how many new customers should be acquired. When they couldn't get a consensus, Kathryn took control and provided convincing reasons why some proposed targets were not the right ones. She decisively set the target of 18 customers by the end of the year.

The team **agreed** that they had made tremendous progress in just two days. More importantly, they **acknowledged** that Kathryn was right all along. They were slowly warming up to her and her approach. Kathryn appreciated this but she firmly said in the next two weeks, she would not tolerate any expression of dysfunctional behavior and she wouldn't think twice of calling out the team if they slipped back to their old ways.

Kathryn knew that things would get worse before they would become better. She also knew that none of them would be surprised if one member was let go. However, they would be shocked to know that it **wouldn't** be Mikey.

PART THREE: HEAVY LIFTING

ON-SITE

Kathryn was not surprised when the progress the team had made in the off-site **diminished**. The team members were still **guarded** with one another and still **wary** of Kathryn's leadership. They were not interacting with one another. Worse, they seemed to feel **vulnerable** because of the things they had disclosed about themselves during the off-site meeting.

Nick called a special meeting to discuss the possible acquisition of the company Green Banana. **JR and Mikey were not asked to join the meeting.** They discussed it in detail and Kathryn held back her opinions so the team could develop their skills in the exchange of ideas.

The turmoil started when Kathryn said Mikey should be in the meeting. Nick harshly said Mikey wasn't going to add any value to the discussion because it was not about PR; it was about strategy. Kathryn did not appreciate Nick's behavior but decided to wait for the right time to call him out.

It was clear that the team members were not keen on the proposed acquisition but it was Nick's **rude** behavior that shocked the team. He told Kathryn that she didn't know squat about the business. This effectively ended the special meeting, but Nick and Kathryn stayed for a one-on-one.

Kathryn didn't mince her words and reprimanded Nick for his mini tirade about Mikey and his behavior towards her. It didn't take long for Nick to spill his guts about being bored and underutilized. He moved his family halfway across the country with the expectation that he would run the company. He also believed that **his colleagues were screwing things up** for the company.

Kathryn asked Nick if he wanted to help the team or advance his career. She emphasized that were not mutually exclusive, but one was more **important** than the other. Nick ended the conversation and left the room.

FIREWORKS

The first official staff meeting went a little dramatic when Nick apologized for being out of line at the meeting earlier. He poured his heart out and told everyone that he made a bad career move by joining the company, but he needed to make a change and wanted to **contribute** to the team. If he could not do this, he said he should leave, but he was not yet prepared to leave. The room fell silent, but Kathryn was thrilled that Nick was staying to make things right.

Kathryn finally dropped the bombshell and told everyone that JR quit but did not provide a clear reason why other than he had gone back to his previous company. When they recovered from the shock of the news, they discussed their next move and collectively decided that Nick was the right person to replace JR.

LEAKS

When Kathryn started having problems with her laptop, the head of IT department Brendan immediately responded. During the short time they interacted, Brendan let out that he wished he was a fly on the wall in one of the off-site meetings because he wanted to **see Mikey answer for her bad attitude**.

Kathryn didn't want to discuss the issue further with Brendan so she changed the subject. In her mind, she knew that she had to talk to the team about **leaking information to other employees**.

OFF-SITE NUMBER TWO

In the second off-site meeting, Kathryn inquired about what sort of things the team members shared with the employees about the first off-site meeting. Everyone admitted to spilling out some secrets to their respective teams, but to varying degrees.

Kathryn then asked the team **where their loyalties lay.** It appeared that everyone was more loyal to the teams they led than the executive team to which they belonged. They understood Kathryn's point. She explained that each member should be clear on who their first team was, which was the executive team. **Their loyalty and commitment should have been to the executive team** and not to the departments they led.

PLOWING ON

Kathryn didn't want to dwell on the issue so she asked how the company was doing. Everyone seemed to agree that the team was moving in the right direction, but Carlos felt they were not talking about the **big issues**. He explained that the engineering team was the **biggest** in the company and perhaps more resources should be allocated to sales, marketing, and consulting. Mikey quickly agreed to the pitch.

Being the head of engineering, Martin didn't appreciate the suggestion, but after being put on the spot, he realized the best way forward was to figure things out and help the company **get out of the rut** it was in.

By some miracle, and after hours of **passionate** discussion, the team agreed on Jeff's **solution** of cutting one future product line and delaying another so the engineers could be redeployed and trained to help the sales representatives with product demos.

ACCOUNTABILITY

With the momentum still strong, Kathryn focused on the immediate goal of closing 18 sales by the end of the year. Nick took over and asked everyone for updates. The lack of progress from Carlos' team prompted Kathryn to talk about **accountability**. She emphasized that some people were **difficult to hold accountable** because they were **helpful** in many ways, just like Carlos. Other people get defensive or are just so **intimidating** that no one challenges them.

Nick then asked everyone to attend the sales training. Since their goal as a team was to close 18 sales, then **everyone** should consider themselves as salespeople. Mikey was not on board with this and shot back that she wanted everyone in the product marketing meeting as well. Nick said if she thought everyone **should** be there, then they **would** be there. Mikey just said to forget it and she would be at the sales training. She added that she didn't want anyone from the team in her product marketing meeting, except Martin.

At that moment, Kathryn knew **Mikey would have to go**.

INDIVIDUAL CONTRIBUTOR

When Nick asked Mikey about the product brochure, she said the brochure was scheduled to go to print next week. Nick said some of the salespeople were **hard at work** doing research for the brochure and they would not be happy to hear that their input was **not even considered**. Mikey didn't appreciate Nick picking on her but she relented and said she was okay with someone from his department adding their suggestions. To make the situation less awkward, Jeff complimented Mikey on the brochure. Mikey said it was what she does best. The **lack of humility** on Mikey's part was the last straw that broke the camel's back. Kathryn could not wait any longer. She needed to have that talk with Mikey.

THE TALK

Kathryn didn't want to prolong the agony so she said flat out to Mikey that she was **not a fit** for the team. Kathryn added that she didn't think Mikey wanted to be in the company at all. Mikey was shocked at what she heard and could not find the words to say. Kathryn felt comfortable that the issue was now on the table.

Mikey was not going to give up and demanded an explanation. Kathryn told her it was her **lack of respect** for her peers and her **unwillingness** to open up to the team. Mikey said the real problem was that the team didn't respect her and they **didn't appreciate** her skills, expertise, and experience.

Kathryn was **firm** on her decision because she believed that taking Mikey off the team was going to help the company move in the direction it needed to go.

LAST STAND

When Mikey got her bearings back, she said she was not resigning and she would not make things easy for them to fire her. Kathryn said she was not firing her and she didn't have to leave, but she had to **change her behavior**. Mikey was not willing to go through with that because she didn't think her behavior was the problem. Kathryn enumerated the times she was rude, disrespectful, and out of line, which stunned Mikey. She demanded an exit package consisting of three months' worth of severance pay, all her stock options vested, and an official record that shows she resigned on her own volition. Kathryn didn't promise anything, but she was okay with her demands.

Before she left, Mikey said the company was screwed without sales and marketing people. She wouldn't be surprised if people from her team left with her. She wanted to **punish** Kathryn for letting her go.

FLACK

Kathryn told the executive team that Mikey was leaving the company because she was **not keen on changing her attitude and behavior.** The team was obviously rattled and started to ask questions about marketing and what to say to the employees and to the press. Kathryn assured everyone that there would be someone from the company who could **step up to the plate**. If the team worked together and **made progress** then there was no reason to worry about what the employees and the press would say about the situation.

Although the team accepted Kathryn's reasoning, the mood in the room changed dramatically. She realized that she had to push the team harder to **focus on the goal** and put the issue about Mikey behind them.

HEAVY LIFTING

Although the team had made progress for the rest of the day, it couldn't be denied that Mikey's departure **dampened the spirits** of the team. Kathryn addressed the group to assure them they could deal with the issue as a team. Kathryn **reassured** the team by telling a story about her first management position job. One staff member named Fred was the most reliable person in the company, but the other staff could not stand him. Kathryn **tolerated** his behavior because of his skills and expertise. However, the output of the department began to slide. Many of her staff complained about Fred. It became clear that Fred was contributing to the problem, but instead of firing him, she **promoted** him. Things got worse and three of her seven analysts quit. The manager fired Kathryn.

Kathryn explained that it wasn't Fred's behavior that hurt the team production, but Kathryn's **tolerance** of his behavior. She drove home the point that she didn't want to **lose the other executives** in the room, that's why she let go of Mikey.

RALLY

The team discussed who would be best to **replace** the head of marketing. There was a heated debate about **promoting** someone from Mikey's team, but it ended in a stalemate. Kathryn decided to break the tie and declared that in as much as she wanted to promote someone internally, the team must search for a new VP **outside**.

Over the next couple of weeks, Kathryn pushed her team harder. She **forced** them all to behave like a team working to reach a goal. The team was **slowly** having a genuine sense of purpose. Kathryn hoped that she could keep it that way long enough for them to see the tremendous benefits.

PART FOUR: TRACTION

HARVEST

In the off-site meeting, Kathryn acknowledged the team for working so hard. They were still behind two of their competitors but they were **clearly on track**. They re-examined the model of **5 team dysfunctions** to help them assess where they were as a team. The discussion proved that they were a better team who could handle conflicts. Kathryn was happy with the progress so far, but she didn't want to make the team too **comfortable** or **complacent** so she reminded them that things would be difficult. They were not yet out of the woods, but Kathryn sensed that with the changes in their behavior, they would soon **reap the benefits of their efforts**.

GUT CHECK

At their quarterly two-day staff meeting, the **new vice president Joseph Charles** joined the team. The most important news of the day was that Green Banana, the company they were considering acquiring, made an **offer to buy DecisionTech**. They were told the offer was a bit more than the company's current estimated value. This meant everyone would get a decent payout. Martin passionately pleaded **against** the offer. Jeff said the board thought it was a **bad** offer.

The board was leaving it up to the executive team to decide if they would agree to the acquisition as a form of gut checking. They wanted to make sure the executives wanted to stay and fight for the company. They all agreed to **vote against the buyout.**

The team then introduced Joseph to the 5 dysfunctions and he experienced how the team operated during a meeting. It was the most intense executive team he had ever seen and he could not wait to be an active part of it.

THE MARCH

In the next 12 months, DecisionTech's sales grew dramatically and **met the revenue goals** for the first three quarters. The company jumped to the number one spot but was tied with its main rival. **Employee turnover eased up** and the **group morale rose** steadily. With the impressive performance of the company, Kathryn decided to trim down the number of executives directly reporting to her to a **manageable five**: Martin (CTO), Jan (CFO), Nick (COO), Joseph (VP-Marketing), and Jeff (VP-Business Development).

With Nick assuming the chief operating officer role, Kathryn believed that it made more sense if Jeff reported to Nick. The team seemed concerned with the turn of events, but Kathryn assured them that it was **Jeff's idea** and it was **best for the company**. This made the team admire Jeff even more.

The Model

An Overview of the Model

Genuine teamwork is still **elusive** in many organizations across the world. The reason why teams **fail** to work cohesively and effectively is that they fall prey to five dysfunctions that cripple a team. These dysfunctions are **interrelated** issues that must be addressed as a whole because **susceptibility** to even just one pitfall can hamper the success of the team.

1. **Absence of trust** among members of the team comes from their unwillingness to be vulnerable. They are not willing to participate because they feel like they are being judged for their mistakes and weaknesses.

2. **Fear of conflict** stops team members from engaging in passionate debate and constructive discussions of ideas. Members are highly guarded and often filter their comments.

3. **Lack of commitment** stems from not having said their unfiltered opinions. They would rarely commit to decisions and would most likely feign agreement just to get through the meeting.

4. **Avoidance of accountability** develops when there is a lack of commitment to a decision. Without this accountability, team members are not motivated to achieve the goals because they don't buy in to the decisions.

5. **Inattention to results** occurs when they put their individual needs above the team's collective goals.

Even if the team exhibits just one dysfunction, it will not succeed in what it's trying to do because these dysfunctions relate to one another and it's **hard to isolate just one issue without affecting the others**. Although they sound simple and easy to solve in theory, it's very **difficult to resolve** them in real business situations because it requires discipline and persistence that many people are in **short** supply of.

TEAM ASSESSMENT

Before finding ways to overcome the dysfunctions that exist in an organization, it would be helpful to first **assess** the team to **identify the problems** and see what areas in the organization need improvement. It's a useful diagnostic tool that will determine the team's level of **susceptibility** to the five dysfunctions. Each member of the team should complete the assessment and then the team should review and discuss the result to **identify discrepancies and implications** to the team's overall performance.

UNDERSTANDING AND OVERCOMING THE FIVE DYSFUNCTIONS

Absence of Trust

Team members must be comfortable with each other even during **uncomfortable** situations. There's a **tendency to clam up** at the thought of revealing something to others because of **fear of judgment.** To build up trust among team members, they should be required to become **vulnerable** to each other but they should be **assured** that these vulnerabilities would not be used to **against** them. Without trust, teams are just **wasting their time** trying to fix and manage behaviors instead of focusing on their ultimate goals. Team leaders can do several activities like personal histories exercises, team effectiveness exercises, personality and behavioral preference profiling, experiential team exercises, and 360-degree feedback, to name just a few.

Fear of Conflict

Every relationship **grows** when there's **productive conflict**. In business, conflict is often avoided at all costs because it usually leads to bigger problems when it gets **out of control**. Teams must be able to distinguish productive conflict from **destructive interpersonal fighting.** With productive conflict, team members are discussing ideas, exchanging opinions, and ultimately finding solutions to the problems.

To overcome this dysfunction, team members must **develop** the **courage and confidence** to **call out sensitive issues** and bring them all out into the **open** and work through them. When team members start to become uncomfortable with the healthy debate, they should be reminded that this is a **necessary evil** and that they should not retreat from a debate without any resolution or agreement or a middle ground.

Lack of Commitment

Teams that cannot not make **clear and timely decisions** are sure to fail. The problem is that teams can only decide if there's a **clear consensus and certainty**. The reality is not everyone in the team would buy in to a decision. What needs to be understood is that team members' opinions and comments need to be heard and **considered**. Not everyone would be on the **same page** but there will be more understanding of each other's views so that the decision becomes an **amalgamation** of everyone's ideas.

Avoidance of Accountability

Team members are not willing to call out their colleagues on behavior or **performance** that could **hurt** the team. They just don't want to engage in difficult conversations so they **cop out** instead of entering the danger zone. To overcome this problem, there should be a **publication of goals and standards,** which clarify what the team needs to achieve and who needs to do what, and how everyone must act and behave in order to succeed. Supplement this with progress reviews and team rewards and you'll find that your team will be working better as a **collective** group.

Inattention to Results

Members have the tendency to put their needs before the needs of the team. Without focus on the **primary goal** of the team, it would be difficult to achieve it. Team status and individual status are usually enough to satisfy some members that other goals are just **secondary**. Team members must put team goals above their individual goals.

One way to overcome this problem is to set a **specific short-term goal** and **publicly declare the results**. Team members who are willing to commit publicly to results are highly likely to **work passionately** to achieve the results. To ensure that the team focuses on the results, their rewards must be tied to the achievement of the result.

CONCLUSION

The Five Dysfunctions of a Team not only succeeds in showing us the **dangerous pitfalls** that plague teams or groups, but it also helps us acknowledge our own **imperfections** as individuals when we behave in a group setting. Team dynamics vary across organizations because of the differences in corporate culture, but all these teams experience one or all of the five **dysfunctions**.

What sets this book apart from other management books is its skillful presentation of complex organizational issues. By presenting a leadership **fable**, the theories, concepts, and **principles** are put into context that makes everything easier to understand. The characters in the fable represent the **different types of personalities** that you meet and **interact** with on a daily basis, so there's the tendency to gravitate towards them and care for what happens to them. It's a **brilliant mix** of fictitious tale and theories to depict real-world **scenarios**. This approach is effective in showing the transformation of an organization and how it ties in with the personal transformations of its executives.

The first half of the book shows that even if an organization is well-funded and has the most talented executives, it can still fail spectacularly if they don't work as a **team**. The executives at DecisionTech had no clear understanding of how teams should operate. They appeared like aimless individuals without a clue of how to resuscitate a dying company. They **unknowingly** did things that hurt the organization because they didn't grasp the importance of **working collectively** to reach a specific goal. It took an old-school CEO and a traditional approach to lead a high-tech company to where it needed to go on the strength of sound theories and principles.

The second half of the book elaborates on each of the dysfunctions and provides a **corresponding solution** on how to overcome the problem. It emphasizes the **role of the leader** in the transformation of the team.

Another important thing that this book effectively communicates to the reader is that **changes cannot be achieved overnight**. It's a long process of unlearning, learning, and adjusting behaviors and attitudes. Even when there's a significant change in the team, it's still easy to **fall back to old ways** of doing things. That's why Kathryn kept the off-site meetings going even if they were met with **resistance**. Holding those meetings was a great way to remind the executives of the five dysfunctions so they would take them to heart and keep **applying** the methods.

This book shows that **great teamwork eludes even the best and brightest teams** in large corporations because individuals in the team don't act with a common goal. Add to that the clashing personalities and different personal agendas, then it becomes difficult to exhibit **solidarity**. If teams can overcome their natural tendencies and behave openly without fear of **judgment** or criticism, then trust, productive conflict, commitment, accountability, and focus on results would not be so elusive.

The Five Dysfunctions of a Team is not only a **compelling** read but also a valuable management **playbook** on how to handle teams and the individuals that make up those teams. It can help **leaders and managers** identify the problems and issues in their own teams, and most importantly, they can have the **tools** to tackle the problems confidently.

FREE BONUSES

P.S. Is it okay if we overdeliver?

Here at Readtrepreneur Publishing, we believe in overdelivering way beyond our reader's expectations. Is it okay if we overdeliver?

Here's the deal, we're going to give you an extremely condensed PDF summary of the book which you've just read and much more…

What's the catch? We need to trust you… You see, we want to overdeliver and in order for us to do that, we've to trust our reader to keep this bonus a secret to themselves? Why? Because we don't want people to be getting our exclusive PDF summaries even without buying our books itself. Unethical, right?

Ok. Are you ready?

Firstly, remember that your book is code: "**READ97**".

Next, visit this link: http://bit.ly/exclusivepdfs

Everything else will be self explanatory after you've visited: http://bit.ly/exclusivepdfs.

We hope you'll enjoy our free bonuses as much as we enjoyed preparing it for you!

Lightning Source UK Ltd.
Milton Keynes UK
UKHW011856210719
346567UK00001B/125/P